About the Land's End

Eleanor Allen

Bossiney Books · Launceston

First published 2003 by Bossiney Books
Langore, Launceston, Cornwall PL15 8LD
© 2003 Eleanor Allen   All rights reserved
ISBN 1-899383-56-5
The map is by Graham Hallowell. Photographs by Paul White
Printed in Great Britain by R Booth (Troutbeck Press), Mabe, Cornwall

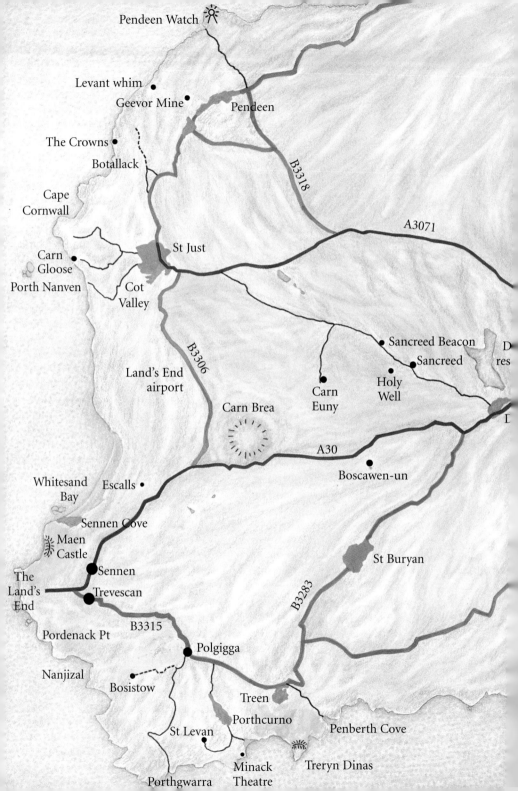

Introduction

There's a strong fascination about standing on England's most westerly point. Spectacular granite cliffs plunge down to jagged rocks and lashing waves, a salt wind buffets your face and all that lies between you and the continent of North America are 3000 miles of wild Atlantic Ocean. It's an exhilarating feeling.

Every year we flock in our thousands – young, old, rich and famous, charity fund-raisers and lone soul-searchers – to sample the Land's End experience. Being part of a tradition – that's an attraction too.

A car or coach might have carried us with ease along smooth, fast roads, but we still get a buzz of personal achievement in having got there – the tip of Britain. The Land's End!

Until the railway reached Penzance in 1859, arriving at Land's End really was an achievement. Cornish roads were too challenging to tempt casual visitors. And even then, travellers determined to make the journey as far as the cliffs of Land's End had to complete the final stage on foot or on horse or donkey-back, because the track was so rough and muddy.

It's difficult to believe it now, but in pre-Victorian times the far south west was thought too harsh and desolate to be picturesque. It belonged only to its inhabitants, who used the sea and land to eke out an existence as fishermen, farmers and miners. The coves were given over to fishing and fish processing, the central plateau to farming, and the north side of the peninsula to heavy industry in the form of tin and copper mines.

And because granite was the only building material available and doesn't easily lend itself to stately architecture, there were no great houses, cathedrals or ornate churches to attract visitors.

From the latter part of the 19th century through to the present day, the Land's End Peninsula, or West Penwith (meaning 'far end'), has had to cope with many changes. Mining has ceased, fishing has declined, farming has been hard hit and motor transport has brought the whole area within easy reach. Tourism has now taken over as the main industry. And there's a lot to entice today's tourist: for such a small area it's amazingly diverse and rich in its scenery, archaeology, industrial archaeology, legend, folklore, and sheer atmosphere.

The tiny fishing cove of Porthgwarra

Tourism is vital to the local economy, but unfortunately modern tourism brings all sorts of problems along with it.

Cornish people and their local authorities are very aware that unsympathetic development, traffic congestion, overcrowding in beauty spots and erosion of footpaths and historic sites all have to be dealt with. The Land's End peninsula in particular is on a knife edge. Attract too many tourists and there's a danger they'll destroy the very spirit and uniqueness of the place they've come to see; attract too few and the local economy will suffer.

The problem is further aggravated by the fact that most people come to Land's End in the summer months, instead of spreading their visits over the year. In fact all seasons have their appeal. Each shows us a different face of Land's End.

In spring you'll see wild flowers carpeting the cliff tops and smothering the roadside verges. In summer all the visitor attractions are in full swing and the beaches are warm and inviting (it's said you can get a tan quicker here than on the Côte d'Azur).

The views from the coast path are always spectacular – dramatic rock formations set against the backdrop of the Atlantic Ocean

In quieter, mellower autumn there are sudden days of glorious warmth. But in winter, when the wind's blowing a gale and the seas are steely grey and raging, or mists are sweeping in and the lighthouses hooting eerily, that's when the old spirit of Land's End re-emerges, with its grim granite remoteness and sense of legend and mystery. It's then you sense that all the changes made in modern life are nothing more than surface trappings and could easily be swept away in the blink of an eye.

The fifteenth century church at Sancreed, with four ancient Celtic crosses and the graves of Elizabeth and Stanhope Forbes, founder members of the Newlyn School of artists

The central area

The direct approach to Land's End itself is along the A30, down the central plateau of the West Penwith Peninsula. The road has been widened and straightened over recent years to speed up holiday traffic, but there's still a feeling of heading somewhere remote. After leaving the leafy suburbs of Penzance you soon notice how treeless this central plateau has become and, even though you can't see it, you can sense the sea is only a short distance away on both sides. Sometimes, too, the weather changes abruptly because the peninsula has its own microclimate. You can leave Penzance in brilliant sunshine and soon find you're plunging into mist, or vice versa. Tourists travelling this road probably get the impression that there's not much to see close by, but two short detours could bring surprises.

At Drift take the road signposted to Sancreed. Immediately there's a really incongruous sight for remote Land's End – a large and picturesque reservoir with swans, and a large (free) parking and picnic area. Drive on and you're passing through old sunken lanes edged by high stone walls, known in Cornwall as 'hedges'. In May and June these hedges are a lovely sight, smothered with wild garlic, bluebells and foxgloves.

The hamlet of Sancreed lies in a sheltered, leafy and timelessly peaceful spot. In the churchyard of the squat little 15th century church are four ancient Celtic crosses and the graves of two artists. Stanhope Forbes and his wife, Elizabeth, were joint founders of the 'Newlyn School' of artists at the end of the 19th century.

Sancreed Holy Well, one of many wells in Cornwall whose waters were (and still are) believed to have curative properties.

From the lay-by where you park for Sancreed Beacon, a clearly signposted footpath on the opposite side of the road leads to the Well. An ancient 'spirit of place' still seems to pervade this spot, drawing a tangible response from visitors in the form of offerings – fragments of cloth or ribbon tied to the surrounding bushes

Artists have always been attracted to West Penwith because of the amazing, crystal-clear light on certain days, when the interaction of sea and granite gives intensity to colours and forms. It still brings artists to live and work here.

Nearby is Sancreed Beacon. This small hill, site of prehistoric remains, is a quick and easy climb and rewards you with a panorama of almost the whole peninsula. Mount's Bay glistens to the south and ahead, on the central plateau, is the imposing 28 metre landmark tower of St Buryan church.

Carn Euny. This remarkable site is managed by the Cornwall Heritage Trust; access is free and, out of season when it's at its most evocative, you might be the only person exploring it

Boscawen-un is a circle of standing stones, with a main centre stone which leans at an angle. This was the ancient site of a Gorsedd, where Cornish bards met to recite and sing. There's a special feeling about this lonely spot too and sometimes you'll find little offerings of flowers on the stones

From Sancreed a short drive through more winding lanes and old farm buildings takes you to Carn Euny. This is the site of an Iron Age settlement. In West Penwith the ancient people built out of granite, which is why prehistoric remains have endured so well – there are more to be found here than in any area of comparable size in Europe.

At Carn Euny not only can you see the layout of the houses, but you can also explore a long underground passage, called a 'fogou' (from a Celtic word for 'cave'), which ends in a circular, domed, underground room. Nobody knows the exact purpose of fogous, but it's thought they could have been used for storage or as places of refuge, or both.

From Carn Euny drive back to the A30. On the left-hand side of the road, and accessible by footpath, lies another atmospheric prehistoric site called Boscawen-un.

Whitesand Bay, one of Cornwall's finest beaches

As you approach Sennen, a hill called Carn Brae rises up out of the plateau. The wind-swept summit has been put to a variety of uses through the ages. It's the site of a large Bronze Age burial chamber and a medieval chapel, and it's believed a beacon used to be lit on top to guide fishermen. The tradition is kept alive today with the lighting of a beacon to celebrate events of national importance. There's a car park on the north side of the hill, if you fancy an invigorating climb. On a clear day you can see the Isles of Scilly.

The next detour is to Sennen Cove and Whitesand Bay, which advertise their attractions too clearly to miss the turning.

After an unpromising start, the road suddenly drops steeply, revealing your first and totally breath-taking view of the sea, with the great sweep of Whitesand Bay to your right and Sennen Cove to your left. The beach which fringes Whitesand Bay is one of the largest and finest in Cornwall, ideal for surfing, windsailing, bathing and sunbathing. A smaller and usually quieter beach, called Gwynver, lies a little further along and is accessible around the rocks at low tide or alternatively you can drive back to the hamlet of Escalls and descend by footpath.

The lifeboat station at Sennen Cove

Sennen Cove was once a remote and poor little place whose inhabitants scraped a hard living out of fishing. During the 18th and 19th centuries the main catch was pilchards, brought ashore in huge seine-nets more than 400 m long and 20 m deep. Seine fishing was a highly skilled and complicated business, involving three boats, two nets and lots of directions from the lookout or 'huer' on the shore. Processing the fish, in buildings called 'cellars', was labour-intensive and comprised salting, layering and squeezing out the oil (not wasted, but sold for lighting purposes) before they were packed into barrels, mostly for export to Italy. There are still boats fishing from Sennen Cove, but the pilchards have long departed these shores and now mainly crab and lobster are caught. You can see the boats and fishermen busy with their pots and other fishing paraphernalia near the slipway at the far end.

But fishing has been dwarfed by tourism, which plies its trade along a smartened up sea front in souvenir shops and cafés, and the fishermen's cottages have become holiday accommodation.

The Roundhouse now houses a good quality craft shop, though it

The Roundhouse, built to house a capstan, now a gallery

still retains the old capstan which once hauled boats up the slipway. Nearby, the large and visitor-friendly Lifeboat Station is a reminder that, despite all the changes, Sennen men still maintain a long and brave tradition with the sea, which in many families goes back generations.

The cliff path to the west of Sennen Cove has some of the most stunning scenery in the whole area and you can walk from here to Land's End, which is about 2 km, just over a mile. (More about that later.)

If the sea, beaches, cliff walks and a holiday atmosphere are what you're looking for, then the attractions of Sennen Cove may turn your short detour into a much longer stay.

Otherwise, return to the A30 and you'll soon reach Sennen, 'the first and last village in England', with its famous First and Last pub. A hostelry has stood on this site for over 700 years.

Both folk yarns and documentary evidence connect the pub, and in particular one notorious landlady called Anne George, with smuggling. Smuggling was rife in the area, and was a useful and popular means of income support for many of the population in hard times.

The First and Last pub in Sennen Churchtown

In 1805 a crowd of 'three or four hundred persons' are reported to have attacked HM Excise men who had captured a huge haul of smuggled goods on Sennen beach, 'with a view to carrying them off'. This was no small-time operation; there were 1000 gallons each of brandy and rum and five hundred pounds of tobacco. In those days the First and Last had a reputation for being 'the resort of all the idle blackguards in the county'. In Victorian times it was from the First and Last that you could hire the horses and donkeys to take you on the final stage of the journey along the old rough track to Land's End.

Nowadays, a freshly surfaced, newly widened, and rather unprepossessing road leads you the final mile, to deposit you at the tollgate entrance to the modern Land's End.

The South Coast

With its deep, lush valleys and pretty little coves, this sheltered area presents a completely different face from the flat, treeless farmland of the interior.

To explore the south coast route, turn off the A30 at a place called Catchall and take the B3283 south to St Buryan (the village whose impressive church tower dominates the central plateau and also acted as a guide to fishermen out at sea). Through St Buryan the road continues in a south-westerly direction until it merges with the B3315 at Sparnon. From there follow the signpost to Porthcurno (to the south).

Eventually the road will descend into a beautiful, leafy valley called Penberth Valley. It's here you should make the first detour to begin your exploration of the Land's End Peninsula's charming south coast.

Immediately after Penberth take the sharp turn left to Treen, where you'll find a large car park at the top of the village. (It is possible to drive part way down Penberth Valley, but there's limited space which is best left for those who can't walk far, especially in summer.)

Penberth Valley is very sheltered, with an almost sub-tropical feel

Descending into Penberth Cove on the coast path from Treryn Dinas

From Treen car park, you can either walk back the short way you came and enter Penberth Valley from the landward end, or you can take the cliff path route (clearly signposted) which descends into Penberth Cove. Whichever way you start, there's a lovely circular walk with beautiful cliff and valley scenery.

Penberth Valley is very green, full of lush and exotic vegetation. Big-leafed plants like giant gunnera thrive here, enjoying the southerly aspect and benefiting from the protection of sheltering trees and hedges. The small meadows on either side once produced large commercial crops of violets, daffodils and early potatoes, but now the valley and its cottages have a rather gentrified air. A clear, rushing stream runs beside the path, to cascade over the rocks and into the sea in the picturesque cove. There's an old wooden capstan and usually one or two fishermen going about their business, fishing mostly for crab, lobster and mackerel. It was a far less tranquil scene when pilchards were plentiful. Then the cove would have been full of noise and the stench of fish oil and tar, with women and children hard at work in the fish cellars, pressing and packing the fish.

The Logan Rock, on a headland called Treryn Dinas, can be reached from Treen. The views are magnificent, but reaching the rock itself should be attempted only by the very fit and sure-footed.

Treryn Dinas (the name means Treen Castle) is also the site of an Iron Age cliff castle, a fortification consisting of a massive rampart of earth and stones protecting it on the landward side

Back in the village of Treen, you'll probably have spotted the Logan Rock Inn. This old hostelry takes its name from a rocking or 'logging' stone that stands to the south-west on a striking promontory of land called Treryn Dinas. It's said of a logan rock, 'a finger's weight can rock it, but a man's whole strength cannot dislodge it'. Not surprisingly, they were held in great superstitious reverence in the old days, and this was the biggest and most impressive of all, estimated to weigh between 60 and 70 tons. So when, in 1824, a high-spirited young naval officer called Lieutenant Goldsmith took along a dozen or so of his shipmates and dislodged the stone as a prank, it caused an outrage. The young man was accused of vandalism, and of doing two local guides out of a job. He was ordered by the Navy to get the stone reinstated, at his own expense. It had only fallen about a metre, but an amazing lifting structure had to be erected, which took months to build.

15

Looking west from Treryn Dinas.

Legend has it that the highest rock on Treryn Dinas, called Castle Rock, was a midnight rendezvous for a group of witches from nearby St Levan.

On moonlit nights they could be seen flying to Castle Rock to brew horrible spells which stirred up gales and caused ships to founder on the rocks below

After four days of manoeuvring and apparently receiving little help from the sixty men recruited from St Just, who 'did little but drink beer' (and still expected payment), the rock was finally put back into place. It cost a huge sum, which is said to have bankrupted young Goldsmith. And unfortunately, despite all the effort and expense, the stone has never rocked as freely as it did before. Now the story seems to attract as much attention as the stone itself.

If you'd like to see what the lifting structure looked like, there's an old illustration of it in the bar of the Logan Rock Inn – as good an excuse as any to pop in at the end of your walk.

From Treen return to the B 3315 and follow it to Trethewey. Here's where you make your next detour. Follow the sign left to Porthcurno. Eventually the road makes a really steep descent into Porthcurno Valley and the view is spectacular. You can easily spend a whole day or more in and around Porthcurno, especially in summer.

Porthcurno Cove's long-established popularity with holidaymakers lies in its lovely, sloping sandy beach, which is south-facing and sheltered by cliffs, making it a perfect place for bathing and sunbathing. There are plenty of parking and refreshment places for anybody wanting to spend time here

The Museum of Submarine Telegraphy at Porthcurno, seen from across the valley

Since 1870 Porthcurno has also been a communications centre, which gives it in parts an efficient, well-groomed feel, alongside the relaxed holiday atmosphere. You might be surprised to learn that telegraph cables which link Britain to the rest of the world run under the beach and out to sea at this point.

The Museum of Submarine Technology, open all year, makes good use of existing resources. It's enterprisingly housed in a bombproof bunker that was tunnelled into the cliff-side to shelter telegraph workers in the Second World War. The museum recreates the wartime atmosphere and anyone fascinated by machines will love all the working equipment, some of which dates back to Victorian times.

The Minack Theatre

After you've had your fill of Porthcurno, take the steep, winding road at the seaward end of the valley, signposted 'St Levan'. At the top, on the left, you'll find the spectacularly sited, open-air Minack Theatre. Here, built into a Cornish cliff-side, is a theatre that looks more like a Greek ruin than a modern stage and whose back-cloth is the wide expanse of Porthcurno Bay. It's a wonderfully romantic place to watch a performance on a summer night, with the stage illuminated against a darkening expanse of sea and sky.

But the theatre's not just open for performances. It's such a famous and interesting place that you can look round any time of year. The visitors' centre explains how it came to be built in the 1930s by an amazing woman called Rowena Cade and her two assistants, with their own bare hands. You can wander down the granite tiers of cliff-side seats, or even go on to the stage area and strike a few dramatic poses for the photo album. If it's blowing a gale, you can sit back and enjoy the same views from a magnificently sited coffee shop. The Minack blends into, utilises, and even enhances the natural scenery in an inspired way. Even if you're not lured back to see a performance, a daytime visit is still a magical and memorable experience.

St Levan church. Inside are some interestingly carved bench ends – well worth a look

St Levan's Holy Well

From the Minack the road runs for about 800 metres to St Levan and little Porth Chapel beach. Atmospheric little St Levan is shrouded in legend and history. There's an ancient church dedicated to St Selevan, a Celtic saint, built with its eastern end set against the steep hillside. Nearby stand a ruined chapel, a holy well and St Levan's stone, cracked in two, the story goes, by the saint himself. There were dire prophecies about the end of the world being nigh should the crack ever grow wide enough for a pack horse with side panniers to pass through. Even the churchyard has a grisly legend, concerning the grave of a certain Captain Richard Wetheral and a ghostly ship's bell. St Levan's a weird and wonderful place, but the approach road is very narrow and it's a dead end. You should really be prepared to leave the car behind and walk there (1 km), especially in summer.

Porthgwarra, famous for its tunnels through the rocks to the beach

Return to the B3315 after your detour to Porthcurno, Minack and St Levan and turn left. Follow the road to a place called Polgigga (not as interesting as its name). There you'll see a sign to a small intimate fishing cove called Porthgwarra. Here is your third detour.

A winding and narrow country road ends right at the cove, by a surprisingly large car park. You can either explore the cove itself or take a walk along the cliff path – back in the direction of Porthcurno, or towards Land's End. In both directions the views are splendid. Porthgwarra is chiefly famous for two things: its lobster fishing and the mysterious tunnels cut through the rock alongside the slipway. The tunnels are so picturesque and intriguing, it's tempting to ascribe a colourful use to them. In reality the explanations put forward are rather mundane. Apparently they were either cut to allow fishing boats to be hauled in when the steep slipway was being pounded by heavy seas, or they were for farmers to take their carts through to collect seaweed for fertiliser.

All the tiny coves and inlets along this south coast were used for smuggling, but Porthgwarra's the one that most looks the part. Some of the young men who farmed inland are reputed to have kept fast sailing boats here at the turn of the 18th century, when smuggling was in its heyday. After the harvest was safely in, they'd take little trips over to France and return with illegal, duty-free wine and spirits and other goodies. Locals shared in their ill-gotten gains and regarded them as heroes. The men preferred to call themselves 'free-traders' rather than smugglers, but it was a hazardous business, with Revenue men for ever on the watch and harsh punishment for anybody convicted.

From Porthgwarra rejoin the B3315 by turning left. It leads you north-west. After about two and a half kilometres, it brings you back to the A30 and the entrance to Land's End.

Strange boulders on the cliffside above Porthgwarra

Pendeen Watch. The sea on calm, sunny days is a gorgeous, sparkling aquamarine.

But don't be deceived. What you're looking at can be one of the wildest and most dangerous stretches of coastline in the British Isles.

In the days of sailing ships and before the lighthouse was built many fine vessels came to grief

The North Coast

The change in character is intense. The north coast has a rugged, lonely grandeur quite unlike the sheltered south. It offers magnificent views of cliffs and ocean, but keeps the sea tantalisingly inaccessible.

Instead of heading due west for Land's End, try heading north-west, on the A3071 out of Penzance, towards Newbridge. Through Newbridge keep going until you reach the B3318, and turn towards Pendeen. You've now crossed the peninsula from south to north, English Channel to Atlantic Ocean, in under 10km.

This area of amazing natural beauty was once a scene of heavy industry. It has been a valuable source of tin and copper from prehistoric times and is dotted with the remains of a once great mining industry, making it a fascinating place for anybody interested in Cornwall's industrial past. The chief surface remains are engine houses, built of granite and growing over the years to look more like ruined castles. The whole area is riddled with old workings, including mine shafts, and should be explored with caution.

Plain, workaday Pendeen, with its rows of old miners' cottages, looks like a place for tourists to hasten through, but it's here you take your first detour.

Take the narrow road signposted 'Pendeen Watch'. After a kilometre or so, you arrive at the top of a cliff, beside a smart working lighthouse. The lighthouse is open to visitors at popular times of year, but you're mostly here for the terrific view – north to Gurnard's Head and south towards Botallack. Try to park to the right of the lighthouse and, if the weather's bad, you can see all this without leaving your car.

Return to the B3306 at Pendeen and turn right, towards St Just. Anyone interested in industrial archaeology will want to take a second detour to inspect the Levant 'whim' engine house. Levant mine once produced tin and copper in greater quantities than any other mine in West Penwith. It also became notorious as the scene of a terrible mining disaster, when 31 miners died. The whim engine house, with working engine, has been restored by the Trevithick Society and The National Trust.

Along the B3306 the grey, granite old mining villages of Pendeen, Trewellard and Botallack merge into one another. At Trewellard is Geevor Mine, one of the last mines in Cornwall to produce tin.

Geevor Mine, which closed only in 1990, after the price of tin collapsed in the 1980s, but is now a successful year round museum and visitor attraction

The Crowns engine houses of Botallack Mine

Your next detour, offering both scenery and mining history, is at Botallack. If you want to visit only one industrial site on the north coast, this is the most spectacular. Turning right out of the village, you pass a striking old Cornish farmhouse, Botallack Manor Farm. Its façade was used as Nampara in the well-loved *Poldark* TV series based on the books by Winston Graham – a reminder that West Penwith has strong literary as well as artistic connections.

Continue past a building called The Count House and park on the cliffs. Already the views are tremendous, but if you walk a little further, you'll see one of the most famous and most photographed views in the whole of Cornwall – the two ruined Crowns engine houses of Botallack Mine, spectacularly sited by the waves at the foot of jagged cliffs. The underground workings stretched right out under the Atlantic and miners claimed they could hear the ocean booming above their heads.

While here, spare a thought for the miners, and women and children employed alongside them. They had to trudge over these cliffs in all weathers, then descend into the mine by a series of steep wooden ladders, before embarking on long hours of toil in dark and dangerous conditions. When the bottom fell out of the tin and copper mining industry in the 1860s, hundreds of miners and their families were

Britain's most westerly town, St Just, is the hub of West Penwith

St Just has more than its fair share both of public houses and of chapels, as befits a Cornish mining town

forced to emigrate. It was said that wherever on the globe you found a mine, you'd find a Cornishman at the bottom of it.

From Botallack continue along the B 3306 to the most westerly town in Britain, St Just. This little granite, former mining town is bare and treeless, but a bustling hive of activity in the summer months. John Wesley, the founder of Methodism, preached here to great effect in the 18th century, when times were hard and lawless, and heavy drinking was a consolation. Wesley's strong and enduring influence is to be seen in all the chapels dotted about the peninsula, two of the largest being here at St Just.

Before starting out on your next detour, why not buy a hot Cornish pasty in the market square, to eat on the cliffs? Cornish pasties always seem at their tastiest eaten out in the open.

Above: This remarkable building is Ballowal Barrow, a Bronze Age 'entrance grave' whose builders used an earlier (Neolithic) structure as its base. It probably had a conical roof and was taller than it is today

The best place nearby for a picnic is Carn Gloose. From the centre of St Just, take the road to Cape Cornwall, then branch left, just after the school. On the way, you'll pass an interesting archaeological site called Ballowal Barrow, which is a large and particularly impressive Bronze Age burial mound. At Carn Gloose you're on the cliff edge and parking is free and informal. To your right lies Cape Cornwall and to your left lie Sennen and Whitesand Bay. The rocks you can see off-shore are The Brisons, the notorious scene of several shipwrecks.

A track to your right from Carn Gloose will lead you on foot to Cape Cornwall, but if you prefer to drive there, return towards St Just and follow the signs. At one time Cape Cornwall was thought to be the most westerly part of Britain, the original Land's End. You can climb to the summit of the Cape, which is crowned by an old chimney stack, or walk along the cliffs and spot seals swimming out at sea.

Once this whole area was extensively mined, but now it's hard to imagine such a beautiful place polluted by all the noise, smoke and smell of heavy industry.

Above: Carn Gloose with The Brisons out at sea

Below: Cape Cornwall, topped by a mine chimney stack and with other evidence of its mining past

Porth Nanven, at the seaward end of Cot Valley

Drive back towards St Just again and from the centre make one last detour by following the road to Cot Valley. The landward end of the valley is a sheltered spot and, surprisingly for the north coast, a little oasis of lush, exotic planting. There's a small stream, mining remains and good views from the cliffs at the cove end, Porth Nanven. This is also the only place where you can easily reach the sea on this bit of coast, though it is unsuitable for swimming.

The boulders here are unique to the area and you're warned not to remove them. There was an outcry a few years ago when some large and magnificent Cot Valley specimens turned up as decorative features for tourists on the promenade of a seaside town in Lancashire!

The detours around St Just end back in the town, on the B 3306. You head towards Sennen and Land's End. On your left you'll eventually see Carn Brae, and on your right, Land's End Airport which offers coastal flights. Just after the airport, the road joins the main A 30 and sends you speeding on the last part of your journey through Sennen and towards Land's End.

A photo opportunity at Land's End. The signpost can be varied to give the name of your home town

Land's End

England's most westerly point can be reached either by walking along the cliff path from Sennen Cove (under 2 km) or by driving through the toll gate entrance to the Legendary Land's End theme park.

If you take the theme park option, you pay just for parking and then all the attractions are pay-as-you-go. Here you'll find a choice of refreshment areas, souvenir shops, a restored farm, undercover exhibitions and spectacular man-made attractions. The Last Labyrinth takes you right down into the granite heart of Land's End and back in time on journeys through legend and history, employing all the latest 21st century special effects.

The theme park is open all year round and there's plenty to do that's undercover, offering hours of amusement for all ages. It also provides year-round work for local people and some of the revenue it generates is ploughed back into tackling the erosion caused by the thousands of feet trampling the cliffs.

It's here, on Land's End itself, that the problems of balancing the needs of the local economy, visitor expectations and conservation of the environment are at their most acute. There's no easy solution.

The most westerly point itself lies beyond the First and Last House. It's called Peal Point or, by nickname, Dr Syntax's Head, after a large, curiously head-shaped rock lower down the cliff. This is not the most spectacular headland along this stretch of coast, but obviously its position makes it the most special and most celebrated.

As you stand on Peal Point, the Isles of Scilly lie to the west. You can see them on a clear day, though locals claim that if you *can* see them, bad weather is sure to follow. The long rock with the rugged outline, sticking up out of the sea, is thought to look like a recumbent knight in armour, so it goes by the name of The Armed Knight. It's home to many sea birds such as razor-bills, shags, guillemots and members of the auk family. The rock to the south, with the natural arch, called Enys Dodman, is home to a colony of greater black-backed gulls.

Out to sea is the Longships lighthouse, whose light first beamed out in 1795. In the channel between Longships and the mainland lie many submerged reefs with colourful names like the Shark's Fin and Kettle's Bottom. To the south-west is the Wolf Rock lighthouse of 1870, which is said to get its name from a howling noise made by waves in a cave in the rock beneath.

Fierce tides, strong cross currents and gale force winds have driven many ships to disaster on this treacherous, shelterless section of coast. Even since the lighthouses were built and modern navigational aids introduced, disasters have unfortunately still continued.

Under the waves between Land's End and the Isles of Scilly lie not only many wrecks, but also King Arthur's legendary lost land of Lyonesse, said to have been submerged beneath the waves by a great flood. There are many romantic tales of fishermen sighting the roofs and towers of sunken villages, and hearing church bells pealing on stormy nights. As you stare out over a storm-tossed sea or a gentle swell stained red by a glorious sunset, it's easy to be swept along by the myth of Lyonesse.

If you decide to follow the cliff path round to the north, you'll be rewarded with much finer scenery than that around Peal Point. The cliffs are flat-topped, covered with gorse and heather and an assortment of wild flowers that have learned to cope with salt and spray. On Mayon Cliff you'll pass Maen Castle, the remains of another Iron Age cliff castle, probably the earliest in West Penwith and dating to around the 6th century BC.

The Land's End complex of hotel and theme park, seen here from Greeb Farm, which is maintained as an educational exhibit

Further along, a tall finger of granite rock sticks up dramatically out of the sea. This is called The Irish Lady. Legend has it that the sole survivor of a shipwreck, a beautiful Irish lady with long red hair, was washed up on the rock. But the seas were so mountainous, nobody could reach her and she died. On stormy nights, she can be seen sitting here, looking surprisingly serene despite her fate.

Next comes the magnificent headland of Pedn-men-dhu where the huer once kept watch for shoals of mullet and pilchard, and signalled noisily to the fishermen of Sennen Cove. Later it became a coastguard lookout. During the Second World War the Marine Commando Cliff Assault Wing trained on these cliffs and today they're very popular with rock climbing enthusiasts. From this headland you descend into Sennen Cove itself.

A walk to the south from Peal Point takes you to Greeb Farm, restored and stocked with animals by the theme park. Continue and you reach the fine Pordenack Point, where the first beacon was lit to warn of the Spanish Armada in 1588 and which, according to legend, was once home to a famous witch called Madgy Figgy.

31

Nanjizal, or Mill Bay

Beyond that (also accessible from the landward side by footpath from Trevescan, Polgigga or Higher Bosistow) is the very beautiful Mill Bay, or Nanjizal. It's here that all the best natural elements of the Land's End coastline combine – a breathtaking bay with a natural rock arch, a sheltered sandy beach, and a big cave, accessible from the beach at low tide. Nanjizal can only be reached on foot and then by a steep descent to the beach, so it remains the preserve only of the more determined few. This idyllic spot seems the perfect place to end our journey about Land's End.

Some other books which may be of interest:
About Penzance, Newlyn and Mousehole, Michael Sagar-Fenton (Bossiney)
About Mount's Bay, Michael Sagar-Fenton (Bossiney)
Ancient Cornwall, Paul White (Tor Mark Press)
Classic ghost stories from the Land's End, William Bottrell (Tor Mark Press)
Folk tales from the Land's End, William Bottrell (Tor Mark Press)
The natural history of the Land's End, Jean Lawman (Tabb House)